an anthology of original poetry and prose on love and modern relationships commemorating the modern love UK Tour 2001

renaissance one

First published by renaissance one, 2001
PO Box 22004, London, SW2 5ZS, England

Collection copyright © renaissance one, 2001
Photographs © Lyndon Douglas

The copyright in each of the pieces in this collection remains with the original copyright holder.
'Androgyny Becomes Her' and 'IMMACULATE' are reproduced by kind permission of the Author c/o Bookblast Ltd. Copyright © Jamika Ajalon, 2001
'I heart Shoreditch' first appeared in *Shoreditch Twat*, 2001

The right of the contributors to be identified as the joint authors of this work has been asserted by them in accordance with the Copyright, Designs and Patents Act 1988.

This book is sold subject to the condition that it shall not, by way of trade or otherwise, be lent, resold, hired out, or otherwise circulated without the Publisher's prior consent in any form or binding or cover other than that in which it is published and without a similar condition including this condition being imposed on the subsequent purchaser.

ISBN 0-9541230-0-X.

Cover design by Sally Mountain
Typeset, printed and bound at Peepal Tree Press

CONTENTS

Introduction	4
2001 **Patience Agbabi**	7
The Manager's Wife **Jacob Sam-La Rose**	8
Monologue **Francesca Beard**	9
Androgyny Becomes Her **Jamika Ajalon**	11
Thought on modern love **Ferdinand Dennis**	14
Floating Rib 9 **Anthony Joseph**	15
Alpha Male **Sophie Woolley**	16
The Past **Roger Robinson**	18
For Melanie **Michael Horovitz**	20
Clasped **Malika Booker**	22
Thought on modern love **Ty**	24
Yo Baby **Charlie Dark**	53
What an Ex-girlfriend said after A Love Poem at a Reading **Roger Robinson**	54
IMMACULATE **Jamika Ajalon**	55
Drums of Passion **Charlie Dark**	57
Yesterday **Arora a.k.a. Skorpio The Nemesis**	61
TEXT **Patience Agbabi**	63
I heart Shoreditch **Sophie Woolley**	64
Fragments **Jacob Sam-La Rose**	66
Once Seen, Never Forgotten **Francesca Beard**	67
Floating Rib 1 **Anthony Joseph**	69
Index of Contributors	70
Index of Pieces	71
Tour information	72

INTRODUCTION

This book isn't about flowers and kisses and walks on the beach. No hearts. Some of the pieces may incorporate some or all of these things. There's no aim to create a new souvenir for Valentine's Day. No plan for a happy ever after.

This collection of original prose, poetry and reflection features thirteen leading artists who are united by a passion for words and its power to provoke, entertain and enthral. The starting point is how they view love and modern relationships. Some have written new pieces, others have chosen to relay a perspective on love at a given time.

The book and tour came from a feeling I had a while back that a lot was being written and said about relationships and love that was negative. Magazines and articles were awash with predictions and statistics about disintegrating relationships, based on the merits and pitfalls of the new man, career woman etc. The debates ensued, the contradictions missed, the humour gone. And so came modern love, a project to capture the thoughts and experiences of love by artists I admired and enjoyed working with.

The contributors straddle traditional and contemporary literature. They bring their own brand of art, their unique style and experiences to the page and the stage. They are keen to push literature and the spoken word out to the mainstream. Taking cues from a myriad of sources – pop culture, visuals, advertising and performance art among others – has given their work a distinctive edge and accessibility. With so many references to draw upon, it's not surprising that they are appealing to a ever widening audience – whether representing British writing world-wide, making poetry relevant and accessible to school kids, giving talks at prisons, libraries and youth centres or recording albums and CDs. They are rapidly and progressively changing the once seemingly static literature firmament.

It's a good time to be in the arts with all the talent, energy and vision present. Through the artists' perspectives comes a sometimes bittersweet, but always redemptive, comic and daring celebration of love and relationships. It's all here!

Melanie Abrahams

Thanks and much love to all the artists on tour. Thanks to all who helped in the creation and inspiration for this book: Diana Gayle, Désirée Abrahams and Hannah Bannister and Jeremy Poynting at Peepal Tree Books.

Patience Agbabi

2001

I'm 30-something going on 15,
know 57 different words for rain,
how to vibrate my mobile ringing tone,
that my bum looks big in my twisted jeans
and how it feels to slide a live oyster
over my pierced tongue
and how to pre-set my video to discover
whether Paul's done stuff with Helen.

I've mouthed the words to twenty thousand love songs
but don't know what love is.
All I know is that at 6am the sun
set twenty thousand diamonds dancing on my skin
and how it felt to close my eyes and kiss
and all five senses sing.

Jacob Sam-La-Rose

The Manager's Wife

I don't remember her name,
but I remember how thin she was.
Pale, with sparse, cropped blonde hair.
Nothing like the glossy women
spread across the pages of the men's magazines
we flipped through when shirts had been refolded
and hangers spaced evenly on rails. Quiet days,
the sales boys would flock around the cash desk,
trying to make sense of the match.
The shop floor agreed, either he or she
had made a mistake. He was a nice guy.
Said nothing of being a few minutes late,
as long as you made up the time. She drifted
into the shop every once in a while, flashing a
      brittle smile
before lunch dates with visiting friends. There
      were rumours
of how much the wedding cost. Laughing,
she'd raise a hand to her mouth, wrist angled
to flaunt a finger, thin as a stiletto heel,
weighted with cool rock - nothing too vulgar,
of course. Even I could see how it stretched him
beyond a manager's salary. Even I wondered
what kept him there, alone some nights
among the empty jackets and jeans, trying
to make the day's figures fit.

Francesca Beard

Monologue

My friend Matt doesn't believe that real
    love exists in the real world.
Everlasting romantic, tilldeathdouspart love -
that only happens to fictional characters.
According to Matt.
To say 'I love you',
according to Matt,
is just a figure of speech, or a lie, or a burp of the
    imagination.
Matt believes you can only truly love 'out of time'.
Real-time love is just selfish.
Like, if you were to say 'I love oysters'
you would probably pass a lie detector test, right?-
assuming you really did love oysters.
But what kind of relationship would that be
    offering the oyster?
And even if it is unegotistical, selfless, pure love -
not, you know, with the oyster,
but romantic human love,
the trueness of that love only lasts
until you or they or circumstances change.
It's only fictional characters who have any free will,
let alone consistency of being.
The rest of us are subject to the natural laws of
    chaos and physical desire.
He says that in any case, you can only truly say
whether you've loved someone,

right at the end,
when there's no longer any possibility of betraying them.
And he points out that in the situation of drowning -
a death quick enough to keep things instinctive,
whilst not instantaneous,
people always have their own lives flashing before their eyes.
They're famously not examining the corners of their heart
with the torches they lit for other people.
This, for Matt, is one of the many proofs
that only fictional characters die in love.
(Apparently, a comforting belief in the after-life
where loved-ones are waiting, doesn't count,
which rules out my gran, who died with my grandpa's name on her lips.
Although, she was pretty much already ruled out
by the fact that she was a total bitch to him while he was alive.)
Anyway, Matt says that real love is an art-form
and therefore artificial.
Except of course, in books and films.
We used to go out, me and Matt - I still love him,
though I'm not in love with him,
I don't have any romantic feelings -
though he is a very romantic person,
in a cynical loner kind of way -
and he's definitely physically attractive,
but I just didn't find him sexy.
I think I'll always have a place in my heart for him
because he's such a piece of work,
the things he comes up with are just unbelieveable,
even for a fictional character.

Jamika Ajalon

Androgyny Becomes Her

love bites

love gnawing

ripping flesh to bits

she grew up a girl

hiding her genitals under small double-leafed

figs

love bites

love gnawing

ripping flesh to bits

s/he

brush you off with a lash of her lid

wash you off with her

she/male tongue

playing the bass with

s/he vocal chords

keeping time with

steps so light its got to be heavy
her exhale
inhale shifted the wind
reflections on a yesteryear of sidelong glances
wave of silences
cutting neatly
a circumcision

which way should she turn
caught by the nose at the clit of a
hurricanE
her chochu/punani/rushing hot sticky lava to
cleanse the nations
her cock erect bursting open the annals of
western intellect
with well crafted contradictions

she grew up a girl
hiding her genitals under small double-leafed
figs in fear of castration
in fear of being found out

in her dreams tonight

her sex sang her a lullaby

so easy to fall in love

with falling in love,

romance a fantasy/a longing

some dark strong legs to wrap themselves

around her and

in her/some

soft ripe nipples/to tempt her lips/some lips tempting

her to penetrate the darkness/a whirlwind of

    naked asses pricks

and pussies

love bites

love gnawing

ripping flesh to bits

Ferdinand Dennis

Thought on modern love

Our modern age encourages a profound selfishness which blinds more people than ever to the need to maintain the balance between giving and receiving love. Their hunger for love is not matched by their willingness or ability to give love.

Anthony Joseph

Floating Rib 9

we were about to have sex
she had a face that had been crying she said she
would not be able to come that she'd used
all her water for tears

Sophie Woolley

Alpha Male

Alpha Male: it could be you.

Here's a list.

Alpha Male: makes T-shirts
Beta male: works in film/television/pop promos and doesn't give a fuck about A, C, D, E, F or G
Charlie Male: in advertising. Wishes he was real.
Delta Male: DJ's (still).
E Male (sorry): takes a lot of drugs.
Fuck: web designer/graphic designer/bouncer/
 and the rest
God: Yes.

Girls! Isn't it time you got pregnant?

Looking for Alpha Male? No, neither was I. But remember gels, time is your enemy and fashion is your friend. It's time to get a baby - and fast. Yes, babies is the new black. Broody is the new attitude. Get a life, get a baby and get motherly! Vogue. Just follow this ten pint Alpha Male Plan Diet to make sure you get up the duff by the right sort of bareback prick: an Alpha Male. Because this time, it's important.

1) Go to the pub. Bricklayers'll do, you haven't got time to piss about. Bloke in a Joy Division T-shirt walks in, straggly bits of hair at the back. Yeah that one. Get him. He makes T-shirts. Cool. He's an Alpha Male.*
2) Have some coke and buy him loads of drinks.
3) It's boring in here so go to Plastic People. He's really arseholed.
4) Take him home and get pregnant off him without a condom on.
5) Your period's late, but its okay, the shag was cool.
6) Definitely got a bun in. Your complimentary T-shirt is getting smaller.
7) Back in the Brickie, the T-shirt maker buys you a lime and soda and you sick it up.
8) You move in together you need him fuckin hell hope you haven't got AIDS.
9) Baby comes easy peasy.
10) Loll about in a nice wine bar on the sofa getting off with each other whilst your baby (which you must christen after its place of conception - so BE CAREFUL, one poor gel had to call her one Bermondsey Chi) slumbers blissfully in a carry cot and you're all happily ever after.

---

* Some of the best T-shirt makers are gay. If you manage to find a gay one, you can skip steps 3-8 and procreate in a much more modern and civilised fashion.

Roger Robinson

The Past

As I look through the antiques market looking at old books, bits of crockery and record collections, I'm keeping a keen eye out for something to buy and then sell on the Internet collector bidding sites. Most weekends I'd spend looking for stuff in old markets. Last year I made 10000 pounds just selling old collectibles on the net. I see a stack of magazines and I look at the first one and it's a football magazine from 1976. I look a few magazines down and I come to a pristine copy of a 1970 Playboy magazine. I continue looking and I find a complete collection of Playboy magazines in mint condition. Every issue from 1970 to 1986 is there. I buy the entire lot for a mere ten pounds. I ride the train home excited. I could easily get 2000 pounds or even more bid for this. I get home and take them out and I can't resist my temptation to flick through a few. I pick up June 1976, and as I look at the centre page the body looks somehow familiar. I read about her, and the playgirl of the month is my girlfriend with her name, birth sign and where she was from. In a confused and angry state I ring her up to find out what's going on. She tells me that she posed for Playboy just to get enough money to finish her last year of University so she wouldn't have to take a part time job to finish her medical exams. I ask her why she's never told me this before and she says because she didn't think it was a big deal, it's just a naked body, what's the problem doesn't it look nice. I put down the phone, look at it again and then look at the centre fold for each month of each year.

Michael Horovitz

For Melanie

You ask me to write
about modern love

For me it's no different
from other love

    -    putting one
and another together.

Putting modern
before love
moves love
into time

as putting love
before poem
moves love
into place.

Putting love
above self
moves love
            back
to Day One

                and forward
to Last Things

and so on
        -   back and forward
to the age-old refrain

that (almost) any

love
    is better
            than none.

Malika Booker

Clasped

I remember sitting on a bed,
your hands in my lap pressing
my thumb into those spongy palms
watching the imprint slowly fill
and disappear.
On my twenty-fourth or twenty-fifth birthday,
I stepped into the house
from the October cold,
you pulled me into the kitchen,
twisted the buttons through tight
button holes, those fingers pushing
and flexing,
then spun me into the center of the room.
I leant into you, tried to cinch my hands
around your waist, link my fingers
the space
more like a child hugging an adult
than a woman her lover.
You unwrapped the red bandana
from your wrist, covered my eyes,
saying *trust me*, asking if it was too tight
you cupped my hands,
lifted them to my waist,
palms upturned,
guess you said
I wondered what you had done
the night before we dined on
cheese and onion pringles
as we had no money for chinese

and I told you I craved surprises
every birthday.
I could hear our breathing,
water dripping from the tap
onto the pile of unwashed dishes,
the drone of the fridge.
you slid something across my palm
tickling, making me giggle,
my fingers curled to feel,
I guessed a chain and you laughed,
untied the bandana,
I looked at a silver bracelet, unusual, expensive,
happy birthday you said clasping it.
I promised never to take it off.
To keep it forever.

Four or five years later,
outside woolworths,
in front of the automatic glass door,
a man looks me in the eye, points down to where
       the bracelet lies clasp broken.
Shopping forgotten,
I rush home and call you, near tears,
begging you to pick up, when your voice answers,
I garble about the broken bracelet,
then I pause.
You are silent.
A woman's voice in the background
asks who is it?
A wrong number you reply.
Sorry I say, fingers clutching the phone,
I stand there look at the clasp and
realise it's broken
beyond repair.

Ty

Thoughts on modern love

Nowadays, I see modern love to be more about the love affair with yourself. I find people striving to have better things in life, such as holidays, mortgages, cars, rather than a partner. For me, right now, modern love seems to be more about people looking after no1 rather than focusing on caring about someone else.

Nobody told me that love could also be a big moody ex-heavyweight boxing champion bouncer ready to kill you. I always had the impression that it was a white swan in a ballerina outfit.

CONTRIBUTORS

From left to right: (standing) Anthony Joseph, Patience Agbabi, Malika Booker, Arora a.k.a. Skorpio The Nemesis, Melanie Abrahams, Roger Robinson; Sitting: Charlie Dark, Francesca Beard, Jacob Sam-La Rose

PATIENCE AGBABI

Poet and performer Patience Agbabi has represented British writing worldwide, both with the British Council and independently. She has published two acclaimed poetry collections, *R.A.W.* (Gecko Press, 1995) and *Transformatrix* (Payback Press, 2000). In 2000 she was resident poet at The Poetry Society and a London-based tattoo parlour. She is working on her third collection, *Body Language*.

on the theme of love and modern relationships:

FAVOURITE FILM: *The Postman Always Rings Twice*

FAVOURITE AUTHOR: Carol Ann Duffy

FAVOURITE SONG: 'Try A Little Tenderness' - Otis Redding

Patience Agbabi

JAMIKA AJALON

Poet, songwriter and film-maker Jamika Ajalon's searing, sensual delivery of poetry and lyrics has won her appearances with the Tony Allen Band, The Urban Poets and French dub group Zenzile. Her award-winning short film *Cultural Skit'zo'frenia* was screened across Europe and the US, along with *Memory Tracks*. Her work has been anthologised in *Wasafiri*, *Gargoyle* and *bittersweet* (The Women's Press, 1998).

on the theme of love and modern relationships:

FAVOURITE FILM: *Bonnie and Clyde* (never a sexier movie made sans sex)

FAVOURITE AUTHOR: James Baldwin (he consistently digs deep in there... a master of portraying complex relationships/love on many levels... always honest, real and to the bone (marrow)

FAVOURITE SONG: A cocktail of Nina Simone, Billie Holiday with a good shot of Coltrane usually does the trick.

Jamika Ajalon

ARORA A.K.A. SKORPIO THE NEMESIS

Arora is a performance poet, rapper and musician. He has devised workshops for young people that draw on a range of art forms including music, dance, audio-visual presentation and information technology. He is well known for his demonstrations of the human beatbox artform. His first musical *Taxi Jam* premiered at the Derby Playhouse in 2001.

on the theme of love and modern relationships:

FAVOURITE FILM: *Umrao Jaan*

FAVOURITE VOCALIST: Lauryn Hill

FAVOURITE BOOK: *Secret of Shambhalla* by James Redfield (Bantam, 2000)

Arora a.k.a. Scorpio The Nemesis

FRANCESCA BEARD

Francesca Beard is a sought after poet on the spoken word scene and performs and writes lyrics for the band Charley Marlowe. She has been a regular contributor to The Guardian's *The Guide* and her poetry has been featured in Dazed & Confused, Yomimomo (Japan) and WordWrights (US). She has two published collections *Cheap – The Millionaire of Near Ideas* and *Chicks Love Me.*

on the theme of love and modern relationships:

FAVOURITE FILM: *Grosse Point Blank*

FAVOURITE AUTHOR: Walter Moseley

FAVOURITE BOOK: Nabakov, *Lolita*

Francesca Beard

MALIKA BOOKER

Malika Booker's engaging performance style has earned her numerous international appearances including Rome Poetry Festival and The World Stories Festival (Dublin). Her work has been published in *IC3* (Hamish Hamilton, 2000) and *bittersweet (*The Women's Press, 1998). She is currently writing *Catwalk*, a play on the British fashion industry to be produced by NITRO in 2002.

on the theme of love and modern relationships:

FAVOURITE FILM: *The Five Heartbeats*

FAVOURITE WRITER: Sharon Olds

FAVOURITE BOOK: *Sassafras, Cypress and Indigo* by Ntozake Shange (Minerva, 1996)

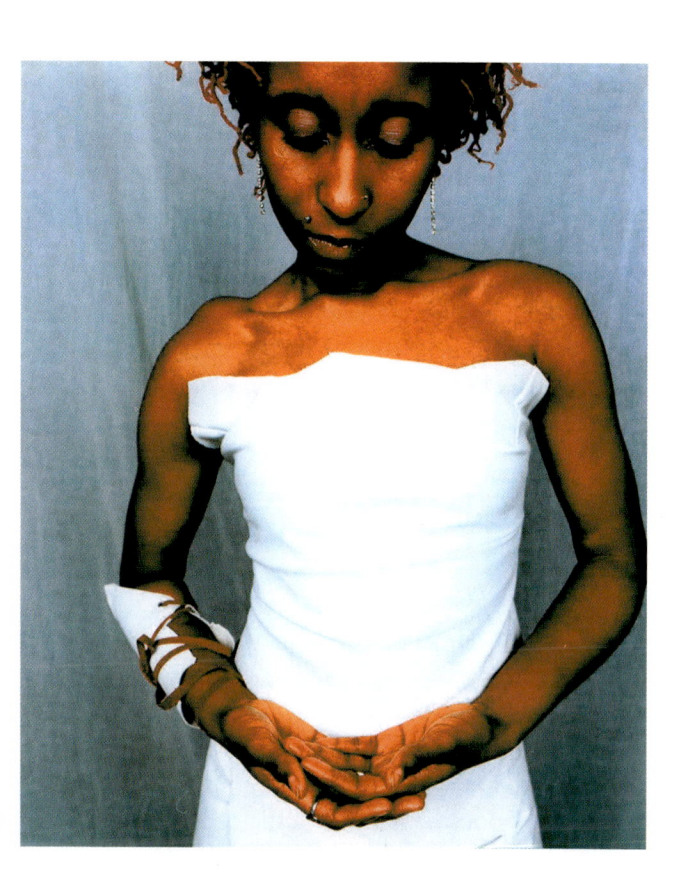

Malika Booker

CHARLIE DARK

With dynamic gestures and vocal gymnastics, writer, DJ and producer Charlie Dark pushes the boundaries of imagery and musicality. As one third of the acclaimed musical outfit Attica Blues, a hip hop inspired trio, he has performed across the globe as far afield as Tokyo, New York and Berlin. He is working on his first poetry collection, *It's Your World, I Just Live Here!*

on the theme of love and modern relationships:

FAVOURITE FILM: *She's Gotta Have It*

FAVOURITE BOOK: John Gray, *Men are from Mars, Women are from Venus*

FAVOURITE SINGER: Sade. Sade. Sade. She is the undisputed master of pain, broken hearts, weeping and wrong doing. My first ever broken heart was healed thanx to the Diamond Life album.

Charlie Dark

FERDINAND DENNIS

Ferdinand Dennis is a novelist and short fiction writer. He is the author of three novels including the acclaimed *Duppy Conqueror* (HarperCollins, 1998). He previously worked in journalism and broadcasting. Dennis's writing has been featured in leading newspapers, magazines and journals including *The Independent*, *Granta* and *The Guardian*.

FAVOURITE SINGER: Nina Simone

FAVOURITE WRITER: Gabriel Garcia Marquez

Ferdinand Dennis

MICHAEL HOROVITZ

Michael Horovitz is a poet, visual artist and singer-songwriter-kazooist. His publications include *Word-sounds & Sightlines: New & Selected Poems* (New Departures, 2001) and *The POP! Anthology* (New Departures, 2000). He has produced many events including Poetry Olympics and Jazz Poetry SuperJam at venues including the Albert Hall and Ronnie Scott's Club, details of which can be obtained via **www.connectotel.com/ PoetryOlympics**

on the theme of love and modern relationships:

FAVOURITE FILM: Almost all of Woody Allen's and *Married To The Mob*

FAVOURITE BOOK: *Collected Poems* by Frances Horovitz (Enitharmon Press, 1995)

FAVOURITE SONG: 'Thank You For The Days' by Ray Davies, sung by Kirsty MacColl

Michael Horovitz

ANTHONY JOSEPH

Anthony Joseph is a poet and novelist and is the author of two books: *Desafinado* (poisonenginepress, 1994) and *Terragaton* (poison-enginepress, 1998). He is working on his first novel, *The African Origins of UFOs*, an experimental work of 'liquid text fiction' and a heady fusion of sci-fi, Caribbean and Afro myths and jazz, an excerpt of which has been published in *Dark Matter: An Anthology of Black Science Fiction* (Warner Books, 2000).

on the theme of love and modern relationships:

FAVOURITE FILM: *Round Midnight*

FAVOURITE BOOK: *By Grand Central Station I Sat Down and Wept* by Elizabeth Smart (Flamingo, 1991)

FAVOURITE SONG: 'There Will Never Be Another You' – Sarah Vaughan

Anthony Joseph

ROGER ROBINSON

Roger Robinson is a poet, short fiction writer and lyricist. He tours with the band Speeka and has been featured on albums including Speeka's *Bespoke* (Ultimate Dilemma, 2001), Juryman's *The Hill* (K7 Studio, 2001), Attica Blues *Test. No Test* (Sony, 2000) and the single *Techno Animal* (Matador Records, 2001). His short fiction book *Adventures in 3D* will be published later this year.

on the theme of love and modern relationships:

FAVOURITE FILM: *The Princess and The Warrior*

FAVOURITE VOCALIST: Roberta Flack

FAVOURITE BOOK: *Brazil* by John Updike

Roger Robinson

JACOB SAM-LA ROSE

Jacob Sam-La Rose is a writer who has performed at venues around the UK, including the Jazz Cafe, Cambridge Drama Centre and the Portobello Festival. He was Poet-in-Residence at BBC London Live. His latest project is as scriptwriter for SlamDunk, an exhilarating dance musical about basketball, beats and brotherhood, which premieres at the NITRObeat Festival 2001.

on the theme of love and modern relationships:

FAVOURITE FILM: *As Good As It Gets*

FAVOURITE VOCALIST: Me'Shell Ndegeocello

FAVOURITE BOOK: *Haruko/Love Poems* by June Jordan (High Risk Books, 1994)

Jacob Sam-La Rose

TY

A spoken word artist, rapper and MC with a world-wide reputation, Ty debuted on I.G. Culture's *New Sector Movement* album. He has been featured on numerous releases and has shared the mic with luminaries such as Talib Kweli, De La Soul and Jeru Da Damaja. He hosts one of London's best-known hip hop nights, Lyrical Lounge. His fêted debut album *Akward* was released earlier this year.

on the theme of love and modern relationships:

FAVOURITE FILM: *Midnight Run*

FAVOURITE VOCALISTS: Ronald Isley, Kate Bush

FAVOURITE SONG: 'At Your Best' - The Isley Brothers

Ty

SOPHIE WOOLLEY

Sophie Woolley is a writer and a performer. Her D.J. Bird Diaries about a relentlessly evil DJ groupie have been serialised in Sleaze Nation. She contributes to the *Shoreditch Twat* and has performed her satirical character monologues at The JAM Festival 2001 at the Barbican and at Sonic Mook Experiment at the ICA.

on the theme of love and modern relationships:

FAVOURITE FILMS: *Happiness* and *Casablanca*

FAVOURITE AUTHOR: Michel Houellebecq

FAVOURITE MUSIC: *Bluebeard's Castle* by Bartok

Sophie Woolley

Charlie Dark

Yo baby

Yo baby! Yo!
If I could rearrange the alphabet
I'd put you and I together!

Roger Robinson

What an Ex-girlfriend said after A Love Poem at a Reading.

Your poems that talk of honeyed winds
blowing round the room are blatant lies!

I was there. What's this shit about sucking
moons from my mouth? Sentimental fool!

Where's the part when I made you beg
to lick me like a puppy lapping milk.

Where's the part when I clawed your back
and the blood bubbled out hot and sticky like tar.

Jamika Ajalon

IMMACULATE

(a conception)

her every trance

her every stance

immaculate

nails cut

just so

skin

red earthglow

immaculate

solid stare

debonaire

im

ma

cu

late

and i want to dirty

her clean white dress

make a mess
on a lush
carpet
So immaculate
feed her fantasies
from a dirty mind
free her pleasure
tease her timeless
and in some
synthesis
some mingled sweat
some stinging tears
some bloodlet years
releasing subliminal fears
the child once born
from this sodomy
some freak duet
is but
raw art
immaculate

Charlie Dark

Drums of Passion

[Cindy Blackmon plays drums with Lenny Kravitz]

Cindy Blackmon played a parra diddle on my heart so powerful I can still feel the repercussions even today.
Boom ba da da Boom!
Crashhhhhhhhhhhhh!!!!
Right, left, right, right, left, right, left, left.
Gucci revolutionary but don't be fooled, just because she wears high heels doesn't mean she can't play drums of passion.
Play the Blues. Lady plays the Blues....
And just because she likes the facial scrub don't mean she can't bring the ruckus,
bring the pain.

Because Cindy Blackmon plays drums like a woman makes love to her man when she's lost the power of speech and sex is her only form of communication.
Passionately.
I mean Cindy Blackmon played the drums that night like a woman makes love to herself.
Rhythmically.
With single strokes
Double strokes

Press roll-pressure roll
Sh,sh,shhhhhhhhh…………….
Delicately stroking Zilgen cymbals
Mother of Pearl!

Deeply entranced by your percussion
Me, myself and every other male in the dance stood riveted as u doubled flamed the snare drum.
Ca..Ca…
Thunder kicked the kick drum.
Bada Boooooooooooom!!!
And tearfully teased our ears with ripples of sound.
My chest was burning with the intensity of your fire
Bam ba da da boom boom, crash, Ba da ding ding tsssssssh, ting
I mean I've seen drummers drum before but this was like a drum workshop for people who can't
Count, Can't dance. Can't listen.
1.2.3.4.5.6.
1.2.3.4.5.6.
1.2.3.4.5.6.
1.2.3.4.5.6.
Have u ever tried tapping your head and rubbing your tummy simultaneously at the same time?
It's difficult, but she made it seem as easy as breathing.

……….
Evenness in rudiments
Sexy syncopation stroking Sabians.

Double flam parra diddles. All that.
4/4. 6/8.
Ever so effortlessly and not a drum machine in sight.
And oh, how the hi hats hissed.
I felt like running up and stealing a kiss.
D.W.
Independence for Jazz Drummers at
www.CindyBlackmon.com
Relentless avalanches of sound and even when your stick broke u carried on playing with your soul.

Seducing sounds ricocheted around the room from her womb as she gave birth to a thousand possibilities.
I want to be that man that makes love to you when the solos finally over.
The one that cradles you at night and whispers "baby, U were good, real good."
Dread locked Super funk soul sister with blisters on her hands.
Master drummer first telephone of man.

I had my chance, the next day in the foyer at breakfast but I could barely squeeze the words out.
The Dark was nervous.
Pshhhh....
I mean what do u say to a six foot sound assassin playing beats u could only dream about?.

"That was nice, really heavy…..
Oh me, my name's Charlie.
And what do I do?
I make beats.

(Here comes the solo)(Solo to end)
Cindy Blackmon played a parra diddle on the heart of the Dark so powerful I can still feel the repercussions even today.
(repeat x infinite to fade)

Arora a.k.a. Skorpio The Nemesis

Yesterday ...

Yesterday ...
I tasted the passion of an exotic gourmet dinner
Under the shimmering glimmer
Of candlelit dreams
Embraced by two beginners
Mesmerised by the starlit skies
In each others eyes
The Gods passed by and smiled

Yesterday ...
I smelt the fragrance of summer gardens
From marigold garlands
The aroma of crisp fried samosa with mint chutney
And mid-morning masala tea
The sacred scent of Sanskrit flames
Mehndi upon honey coloured skin
The commitment of two names

Yesterday ...
I felt the silky heat beneath satin sheets
The wanton yes betwixt laden breath
Moistened lips with tongues a twist
The featherlike stroke of fingertips
The naked grip of snaking hips
Liquids mix amidst a mist of perspiration
The art of creation

Yesterday ...
I heard the cry of tiny tears
Pierce the peaceful night
The shuffle of sleepy feet
The sucking silence
As little lips suckle
A playful chuckle
Ssssh!

Yesterday ...
I saw the wisdom of a grey haired couple
In traditional Indian dress
Bless the wild supple roots of the youth
The truth of their beautiful lives
Personified in their symmetrical flow of words
Undisturbed by ego or vanity
Simple spiritual humanity

Yesterday ... when we kissed...

Patience Agbabi

TEXT

Modern love is in the post,
text substitute for sex.

Substitute sex for love
in dead text.

Sex is with love,
modern is with post.

Modern is in love with post.
Text sex is in.

Post is dead.
Modern is post love.

Sex is the love substitute,
dead modern

Love is postmodern.
Love is dead.

Sophie Woolley

I heart Shoreditch

I love Shoreditch, its great. I like standing in the Mother Bar, glass in hand, lady's cigar in other, watching the fashionable people dancing at a cool party. They are so beautiful, I could stare them out forever.

I perch on a sofa's arm and eavesdrop on a long titian haired girl in a glittering Chloe halterneck top with plunging neckline and ribbed chest offset with ironic gold neckwear. She is speaking to a sculpted bearded designer in Evisu jeans as he primps his passé Buddha hair. The girl says, "Whose party is this?" and he nods vehemently. They talk about a disagreeable sounding mutual acquaintance named Pete who is apparently rude, stupid, selfish, arrogant and tries far, far too hard.

I introduce myself to them as someone they met at that party the other week and then join in their character assassination. I make up lies about things this malign Pete has done, he really is a weird bloke - but I feel sorry for him I say. It's not his fault I'm so fucking marvellous. The ribbed girl talks to me for about twenty minutes after that. For twenty glistening minutes she says nothing of consequence. She is gorgeous.

My boyfriend arrives, fresh faced from riding over from his studio on his scooter. He speaks to a couple of people before coming over. My boyfriend is really handsome and popular. He is rich and lightly tanned. Funny and clever. Well toned under Maharashi. He is everything you could ever want from an EC1 male. I am so lucky, I think as he crosses the room. I am almost crying with happiness. Or maybe it's just the hayfever and the pill I took at dinner. I say something witty and my boyfriend grins and wiggles his tail like a dog.

He looks deep into my shallow heart and we leave quickly. Back at the flat we snort cocaine and fuck hardly with Les Rhythms Digitales turned up really loud. After that he licks coke up me until I come endlessly. I almost break his neck between my thighs, but I can't help it, I just can't stop. Endless, for fifteen minutes. He really is quite something.

Up on the roof garden afterwards I lie on the sloping skylight. Shoreditch Church squats, Old Street hums, bars close for the night. The stars look down on me. I love Shoreditch, it's great.

Jacob Sam-La Rose

Fragments

There is the danger, of course, that nothing is new.
That I only remind you of something you used to know,
an echo of something else you may have wanted, once
    - another him, perhaps.

The way one would catch your breath with a stunning kiss;
a scent you've known, daubed at my wrist or neck;
the way your spine curves to meet the need
    of the body curled behind you.

Perhaps I am a collection of all these things.
A patchwork of familiar fragments.
A note in my voice, reminiscent of a song you loved
    but have forgotten how to name.

Have my fingers traced the same curious paths
    as others that know the glazed skin
        of the thin scar on your left thigh?

Does the way you arch your back belong to me?

Francesca Beard

Once Seen, Never Forgotten

Walking across the damp lawn,
with its hidden fishbones.
I kissed the ribs of your teeth.
In your eyes, the hooks came out, shining.

I wonder if you still search for the next day,
the part in my dream where I say
'We are light pouring through cells'
and you reply -
'Come, we will look for your shoes'.

Since you left, my heart is a cracked pot,
where weeds can grow.
Let's have a resurrection in the thirties.
I would like to undertake your inventory.
Cave mouth seeks wet blur
with a possible view to the ocean.
Self-doubting child WLTM
snake-eating monkey
to climb impervious cliff-face.
Photo appreciated/required/returned
with thanks/stains/derision.
Distance no object.
I have a great recipe for humous.
I have a great sense of humiliation.
My psychiatrist says I'm good-looking.

My friends say I'm a loner.
I have no friends.
I live with my mother.
I've never done this before.
I'm a professional; solvent.
I'm into solvents.
I am the lost pet notice.
Are you my high-low ace?
Distance no object.
Recall me: My favourite colour is 2.
My lucky number is you.

Anthony Joseph

Floating Rib 1

Gravity has few practical applications/ negative
       charge and the pro \\tons
A positive] suppose   I have 2 space ships
-direction of the radius suppose/
                I have 2 spaceships
That's the thing about change
       -hydrogen-
        -foam carbon7.~2 million volts

-the source is a filament the barriers tungsten-
-geophysical prospecting in important places-
many experiments exist][protons and anti-
      particles in a box of gas ~
physical law-   2 spaceships

INDEX OF CONTRIBUTORS

Patience Agbabi	7,26,62
Jamika Ajalon	11,28,55
Arora a.k.a. Skorpio The Nemesis	30,60
Francesca Beard	9,32,66
Malika Booker	22,34
Charlie Dark	36,53,57
Ferdinand Dennis	14,38
Michael Horowitz	20,40
Anthony Joseph	15,42,68
Roger Robinson	18,44,54
Jacob Sam-La Rose	8,46,65
Ty	24,48
Sophie Woolley	16,50,63

INDEX OF PIECES

2001	7
Alpha Male	16
Androgyny Becomes Her	11
Clasped	22
Drums of Passion	57
Floating Rib 1	68
Floating Rib 9	15
For Melanie	20
Fragments	65
I heart Shoreditch	63
IMMACULATE	55
Once Seen, Never Forgotten	66
The Manager's Wife	8
Monologue	9
The Past	18
TEXT	62
Thought on modern love (Ferdinand Dennis)	14
Thought on modern love (Ty)	24
What an Ex-girlfriend said after A Love Poem at a Reading	54
Yesterday	60
Yo Baby	53

TOUR INFO

modern love tour 2001

Love is dead.

Nine leading poets on the international spoken word scene and guest artists present new perspectives on love and modern relationships in a UK-wide tour.

Featured artists:

Patience Agbabi
Jamika Ajalon
Arora a.k.a. Skorpio The Nemesis
Francesca Beard
Malika Booker
Charlie Dark
Anthony Joseph
Roger Robinson
Jacob Sam-La Rose

and special guests

Judith Bryan
Bernardine Evaristo
Ruth Forman
Linton Kwesi Johnson
Dorothea Smartt
Ty
Imani Uzuri

TOUR DATES 2001

2 October	Borders, Oxford Street, London W1
3 October	Arts Picturehouse, Cambridge
5 October	The Gatehouse, Derby
6 October	Kuumba Project, Bristol
9 October	Peterborough Library
11 October	Oldham Library, Oldham
12 October	Maldon Library, Essex
15 October	Essex Poetry Festival, Brentwood Theatre
24 October	Off The Shelf Festival, Centre for Popular Music, Sheffield
26 October	Chesterfield Library
30 October	Luton Central Library

---

18 December Queen Elizabeth Hall
FINALE   South Bank, London SE1

Featuring Arora, Jamika Ajalon, Francesca Beard, Malika Booker, Charlie Dark, Anthony Joseph, Roger Robinson, Jacob Sam-La Rose and special guests Ty and Imani Uzuri
DJ: Acyde
Original music produced by Tony Nwachukwu
Creative Director: Arlette George
Set Design: Lisa Lillywhite
Musical Director: James Yarde

Tour supported by: East England Arts, Cambridgeshire County Council, Luton Borough Council, Peterborough City Council, Essex County Council, LIPPEE Steering Group, Royal Festival Hall and the participating venues.

renaissance one is an artists management agency representing international poets and novelists for bookings. It has produced spoken word events and happenings at venues such as at Borders and The Cobden Club and has worked collaboratively on festivals and tours with the British Council, Miami Book Fair International and numerous publishers. It produced the bittersweet tour 1999/2000, a tour of ten contemporary black women poets, which toured to venues in the UK, Italy, Ireland and the US.

renaissance one